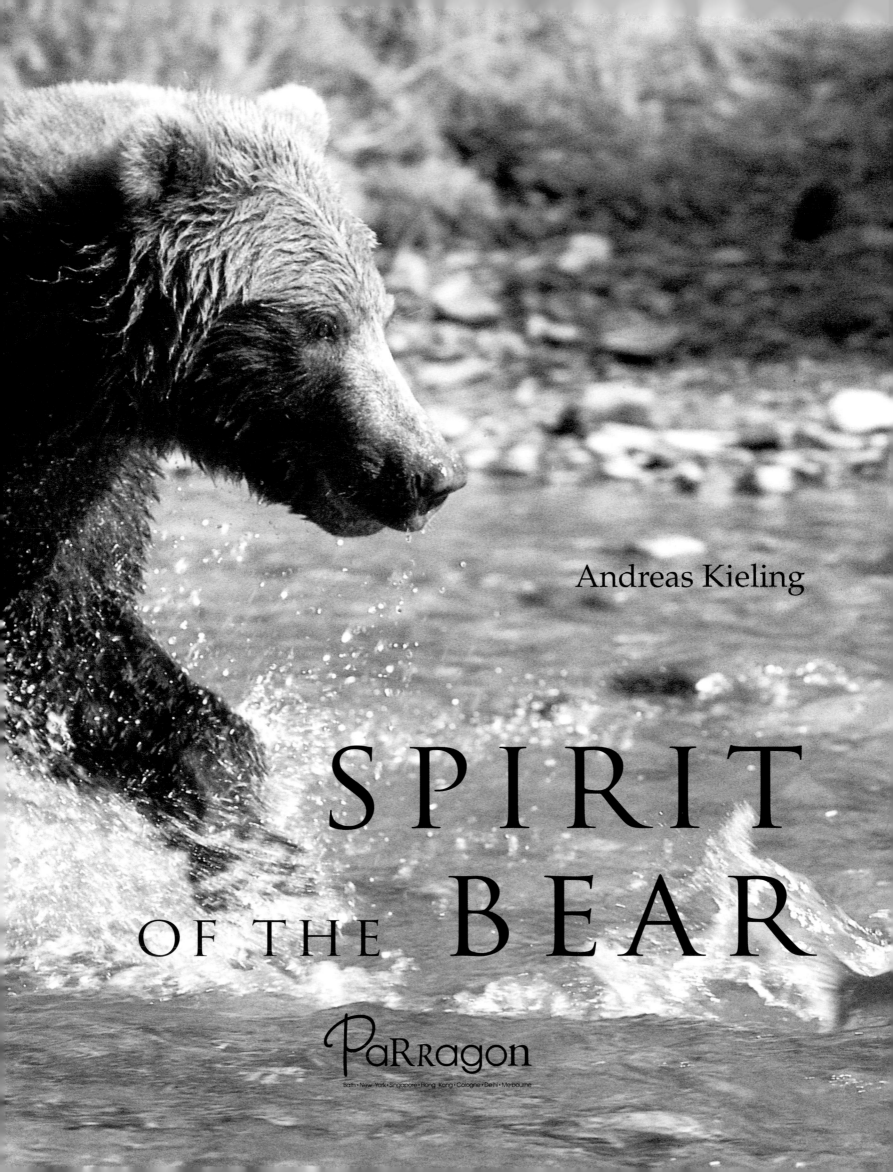

Andreas Kieling

SPIRIT
OF THE BEAR

PaRragon

Bath · New York · Singapore · Hong Kong · Cologne · Delhi · Melbourne

CONTENTS

BEARS ON CAMERA

In the spring of 1991, I saw my first grizzly in the wild on the Yukon River in Alaska. I was awestruck and terrified at the same time; I scarcely dared to breathe. The bear was standing in a large clearing about 200 yards away from me, enjoying a taste of the first fresh grass of the year. What I didn't yet know was that after hibernating for six to seven months, bears are still quite sluggish. Since they need to get their metabolism going again, they have nothing on their minds except the search for food. Everything I knew about brown bears at that time I had learned either from books or from my Native American friends. In their eyes, bears are superior beings, almost godlike—extremely dangerous and impossible to defeat. They kill human beings, plunder their camps, and compete with hunters for their prey.

All of these images flashed through my mind as I slowly crept toward the grizzly, my knees wobbling. He sniffed suddenly in my direction, but then continued his leisurely grazing. The closer I came to the bear, the more nervous and excited I became. I started taking pictures. The sun was low in the sky, a magnificent light for photos—if they turned out to be in focus; my hands were shaking from excitement. But neither I nor the clicking of my camera seemed to disturb the bear. Finally, I came so close to him that I thought this must be a tame bear. I had no other explanation for the fact that he was not afraid of me. Today, after many years of working in close proximity to these animals, I realize that the bear was this relaxed in my presence only because it had never had any negative experiences with human beings.

My second encounter with a grizzly bear was less amicable. In a broad valley in the northern part of the Brooks Range in Alaska, I lay facing the wind with my camera, well camouflaged beside a boulder, when I saw a bear approaching me. It was 300 yards away— too far to get a picture. Then 200 yards, 100 yards—I started to shoot, using a very quiet single-lens reflex camera that I had wrapped in polar fleece to further muffle the sound. Fifty yards, 30 yards—I kept snapping photographs. Suddenly the bear moved into attack position, snorting and growling. It could not have caught my scent when I was facing the wind, but it must have sensed my presence or heard the clicking

A female bear with her two youngsters (*below*), two and a half years old. The cubs are almost as big as their mother by now. I have been acquainted with this female for eleven years, during which time she has raised three litters of cubs.

I have encountered this male bear (*right*) repeatedly over the years; he is about fourteen to sixteen years old. Even when he reached sexual maturity, he was never aggressive toward me.

of the camera. At that moment, I instinctively did the right thing: I revealed myself. I stood up and shouted, "Hey, bear, here I am!" He clapped his jaws together twice, snarled loudly—then fled into the bushes.

Ever since then, I have approached bears openly. Instead of hiding or creeping up on them, I behave as conspicuously as possible. I even wave my arms when I see them from far away, and I make sure that they catch my scent early on. Many animals simply retreat; others treat me with indifference, or they come a bit closer to get a better look at me—but then they go on about their business, hunting for blueberries or other tasty treats, or they return to their caves. I let the bears become accustomed to my closeness over a period of weeks so that they begin to feel comfortable in my presence. Bears can very quickly learn to recognize people by their scents and their voices, so I always speak to them softly.

I also had to learn never to look a bear in the eyes for too long, even the ones I know well. In their language this is a provocation, and it may cause a bear to react aggressively. Something similar can happen if you come too close to a bear with a camera; apparently the camera lens looks something like an eye to them.

In all these years, I have only been violently attacked by a bear one time. It happened during the mating season. An older male had been pursuing a young female for several days. He pestered her relentlessly, but each time she managed to elude him. One day I saw the same female mating with a young male. All of a sudden, the older male appeared in the distance, caught the scent of the other two bears, and ran toward them. The couple sprang apart from each other, and the only creature left standing in the meadow—with a camera and tripod—was me. Instead of chasing after the female bear, the old male ran straight for me.

I shouted at him, but he didn't react; the bear attacked me. At the last instant, I turned around, pulled my head down between my shoulders and presented my back to the bear. Thanks to my heavy backpack, loaded down with technical equipment, I was somewhat protected. At the same moment, I felt a violent blow to my back, and I was thrown six feet into the air. I expected the bear to strike again, but he simply ran away, snapping his jaws and snarling. Perhaps he had the feeling he had gone too far, because in the days that followed, he retreated whenever he saw me. Several years have passed since this attack, but the bear avoids me even today.

Part of my fascination with photographing bears lies in the fact that I have developed real relationships with some of the individual animals. They recognize me when I return to Alaska or northern Canada in the spring, and their trust is evident from the relaxed atmosphere between us.

If brown bears (*above*) are unable to catch the scent of an unfamiliar object, they will often stand on their hind legs in order to get a better view. This behavior is frequently interpreted as aggression. In my experience, however, it is more likely to be curiosity or uncertainty.

Animal photographers (*left*) are considered to be the embodiment of patience. They will often wait for days to capture a subject at its best. If you observe bears over a long period of time, one thing becomes more and more evident: every theory will eventually be disproved, and anything is possible.

Far out on the Aleutian Islands (*following pages*) I often have to pull my canoe upstream for miles in order to reach the salmon spawning grounds. Every year, the Kodiak bears gather here, where they can feed on the highly nourishing fish for several weeks. Occasionally I am followed by individual bears whose destination is the same as mine.

11

What at first appears to be an attack on me turns out to be an all-out battle between the bears over a salmon. Incredible scenes often take place directly in front of my camera, and I have to be careful that the enraged adversaries don't run right over me. In all my years of living together with the brown giants, I have never been physically injured in a situation like this. Disputes between brown bears over a single prey or an abundant fishing ground can often be extremely violent. In autumn, when the bears instinctively sense that that they still lack sufficient fat reserves for their winter rest period, these fights can be observed especially often. At the same time, dominance and hierarchy are also at stake in such confrontations—in this case, between two not particularly strong females. The animal at the left of the picture is the two-and-a-half year old cub of the lighter colored female.

BEARS ON THE LOOSE

There are very few predators in the world that are as adaptable as bears, or that have been able to make their homes in such widely varying environments, from the barren Arctic tundra to the Mediterranean climates of the southern latitudes. Brown bears can even be found on the outskirts of the Gobi Desert. Bears once ranged all across North America, but human beings have driven them out.

Three main factors contribute to bears' widespread proliferation. As the world's largest land-dwelling predator, bears have no natural enemies—except humans. At first glance, a bear's teeth look like the classic dentition of a predator, but unlike those of purely carnivorous animals, the molars are flattened and thus ideally suited to grinding vegetable matter. And like people, bears have the robust stomach of an omnivore.

In Alaska, Siberia, and the northern regions of Canada, bears' diet is up to 98 percent vegetarian; they feed on grasses, flowers, roots, seeds and berries. In the Carpathian Mountains—to the dismay of local farmers—bears happily feed on corn and grain as well as wild cherries and plums, and in preparation for winter, they stuff themselves with acorns.

Brown bears in the coastal regions of Alaska and on the Kamchatka Peninsula nourish themselves mainly with salmon, mussels and fresh sea grass. Bears can also convert sugars from fruit and starches from grains and acorns into fat, but they would need to consume enormous amounts of them to store enough fat for the winter.

Bears are not only all-around eaters who take advantage of every possible source of nourishment, they are also quintessential opportunists. They can feed exclusively on grass, roots or fish for as long as an entire year and still thrive. If a bear locates a source of food in a place where it is not disturbed, it will often stay in the same spot for weeks at a time, moving on only when that food source has been exhausted.

Hibernation (or denning) in bears differs from that of true hibernators, such as groundhogs and hedgehogs, because bears' breathing and heart rates are reduced to a lesser degree and their body temperature drops by just a few degrees. Bears can awaken from their winter sleep at any time, whereas the true hibernators require several days to do so.

By the end of their first summer (*below*), well-nourished young Kodiak bears, who are not more than nine months old by then, can weigh up to 120 pounds (55 kg).

When I anchor my sailboat (*right*), the *Tardis*, in a fjord that is well populated with bears, the grizzlies will often swim right up to the boat. On a few occasions, individual bears have even tried to climb into the sailboat, lured by the "exotic" scents emanating from it.

North and South America are home to four species that belong to the genus of "true bears" (*Ursus*). Three of these are depicted in this book: the North American brown bear (also known as the grizzly), the American black bear, and the polar bear. The fourth large species of bears that live on the American continent are the spectacled or Andean bears. This species exists only in South America, whereas grizzly, black and polar bears are found in North America.

The North American brown or grizzly bear (*Ursus arctos*; *arctos* is the Greek word for bear) grows to a height of 35 to 60 inches (90–160 cm) at the shoulder. The heaviest subspecies, weighing up to 2,000 pounds (900 kg), is the Kodiak bear, named after its geographic habitat on the Kodiak archipelago on the southern coast of Alaska. Standing on their hind legs, the largest specimens are over 10 feet (3 m) tall. With the exceptions of western Canada and Kamchatka, Alaska has the largest brown bear population in the world. The brown bears that live in other regions weigh quite a bit less: in southern Europe, their average weight is only about 330 pounds (150 kg). Worldwide, there are approximately 185,000 to 200,000 brown bears still living in the wild. In Asia, the brown bear's range extends from northern Siberia through the Himalayas all the way to Iran. In addition, southern and eastern Asia is home to other large bear species such as the sloth bear, the sun bear, the Asian or Tibetan black bear, and the giant panda.

With a shoulder height of approximately 35 inches (90 cm), the American black bear (*Ursus americanus*) is smaller than the brown bear and significantly lighter. The average female weighs about 175 pounds (80 kg), while males average around 480 pounds (220 kg).

American black bears live primarily in Canada and Alaska, but they can also be found in the Lower 48 states. Small populations also exist in Mexico. American black bears venture into the open countryside—the habitat of the brown bear—only very rarely. Since their flesh is highly nutritious, they would be a welcome meal for a grizzly bear.

The northernmost representative of the large bears is the polar bear (*Ursus maritimus*). Adult males can

reach a shoulder height of up to 5 feet (160 cm); their average weight ranges from 900 to 1,300 pounds 420–600 kg). Depending on their nutritional level, females weigh between 330 and 660 pounds (150–300 kg). These lords of the Arctic are a prime example of bears' ability to adapt to hostile environments—in

this case, the drift ice region of the northern Arctic Ocean. The polar bear is the youngest species of predator in the world. Approximately 200,000 years ago, polar bears evolved from a population of northern grizzly bears that was probably isolated by glaciers during the last cold phase of our Ice Age.

In the Far North, there is no long transition period between summer and winter. Over the course of just a few days, the leaves change color and fall from the trees. If brown bears can no longer find enough to eat and begin to expend more calories than they can take in, they will quickly retreat to their dens for their winter rest.

Every summer, some female bears in search of highly nutritious seabird eggs (*left*) or chicks swim across to the Aleutian Islands off the coast of Alaska, which are otherwise free of predators, to plunder the nests. This young sow and her cub are systematically searching the island for bird nests. Since seagulls do not nest in holes, most of their clutch falls prey to the bears. Due to the short duration of the Arctic summer, many species of birds are not able to lay eggs a second time in one year.

*Bear families roam across
the same territory over and over,
in search of anything edible.
The home range of
any given animal
can extend from
75 to 200 square miles
(200–500 km²).*

Like many of Alaska's Kodiak bears, this female and her two cubs regularly patrol the shoreline in search of something to eat. Bears can feed on both plant and animal material. Particularly in the spring, before the great salmon migration begins, they often find edible flotsam along the coast.

Bears that live in alpine regions (*following two pages*) often have remarkably light-colored coats. Their fur gradually becomes bleached from the twenty-four hours of light in the Arctic summer and the intense UV rays. In North America, inland-dwelling brown bears are called grizzlies—named for their gray-tipped or "grizzled" fur.

The color of a bear's coat may change over the course of its development from cub to adult. Nearly white grizzlies (*above left*) are very rare, however. This juvenile, approximately seventeen months old, is conspicuous with its very light-colored fur. It is not a true albino, though, since it lacks the characteristic red eyes and pink nose. Brown bears' coats can vary widely in color, from blackish-brown to light buff (*below left and above*). In some coastal regions, reddish fur is quite common.

When she was young, this female bear visited the same seabird island and plundered nests with her own mother. Now she is showing her six- or seven-month-old cub the best spots for hunting. When the little bear grows up, she will pass on the knowledge and behavior she has learned to her own offspring. If a mother and an adult daughter meet each other by chance, the younger bear will humbly retreat and allow the older sow to feed at the best spots. Familial relationships between bears dissolve by the time the young animals reach sexual maturity. Then even close relatives can become bitter enemies.

Shortly before their winter rest begins (*right and following pages*), individual Kodiak bears may be so well fed that they weigh up to 2,000 pounds (900 kg). In order to achieve such a weight, they must have access to a diet rich in fat and protein over a long period of time, the climate must be mild, and the denning period not overly long. Naturally, genetic disposition also plays a role here, and not every Kodiak bear grows to such giant proportions.

Black bears prefer to live in wooded or bushy areas; they avoid open stretches of land. Even adult bears are still good climbers, and they often flee into trees when threatened.

In contrast to the habitat of the brown bear, that of the American black bear extends throughout North America. The desert areas of the outhwest and the far northern sections of Canada and Alaska are the only places where there are no black bears to be found. Thanks to their smaller size and adaptability to human civilization, a wider range of environments is available to them. As far as food is concerned, black bears are absolute omnivores. Insects, small amphibians, lizards, fish, small mammals and carrion, as well as fruits, berries, nuts, roots and grasses comprise a large part of their diet. In the traditional grain-farming regions of Canada and the

The American black bear is the most common and wide-ranging large bear in North America. Its population is not in danger; on the contrary, thanks to the disappearance of its greatest enemy, the grizzly bear, from large areas of the continent, black bear populations have actually grown in recent decades.

Some Native Americans say that the only predictable thing about a black bear is its unpredictability. In fact, black bears are less timid around human beings than are brown bears. The much higher frequency of conflicts between humans and black bears is probably due to the fact that in North America, their range quite often overlaps with human civilization.

United States, black bears cause a substantial degree of crop damage every year. Bears have even become a problem in some American national parks and suburbs. Their keen sense of smell lures them to campgrounds and cars in search of food. In beach areas, it is the garbage cans and dumpsters that seem to hold a magical attraction for bears. In some cases, the bears become so intrusive that unfortunate incidents can occur.

Depending on their geographic range, black bears can display a variety of fur colors. Along with the primarily black-colored bears, there are bluish-gray glacier bears, reddish-brown cinnamon bears, and nearly white Kermode bears.

The primarily black coat of the American black bear is not the only way it differs from the brown bear. With an average weight of 440 pounds (200 kg), it is also significantly smaller. In addition to its smaller size, the black bear also lacks the prominent neck muscles or "shoulder hump" seen in brown bears. The black bear has a flatter brow, and the claws on both its front and back paws are shorter. Even today, the bearskin caps that are part of the dress uniform of a number of British regiments are made from the fur of Canadian black bears. Canada and the United States are also the largest exporters of bear bile to South Korea, China and Japan, where it is reputed to be extraordinarily effective in their traditional medicines.

Although black bears (*above and right*) generally live as loners, groups of them can be found at particularly abundant feeding areas, such as this one at Annan Creek on the west coast of Canada. During the spawning season, they hunt for the highly nutritious fish in the countless salmon-filled rivers of North America just like their cousins, the brown bears.

Pursuit is futile!

Black bears are born climbers and often use this skill

to escape impending danger—for example, an attack by an earthbound brown bear.

Since their geographic range is so wide, black bears live in vastly differing habitats. These excellent climbers have powerful, strongly curving claws. They regularly ascend trees (*left*) to plunder birds' nests or feed on forest fruits.

Like human beings, black bears place the entire soles of their feet on the ground when they walk or run (*above*). They can achieve very high speeds over short distances, and they are also remarkably good swimmers.

The polar bear's range extends across the entire drift ice region of the northern Arctic Ocean. In these areas, the white bears spend most of their time on ice floes, which are kept in motion by the wind and the ocean currents. Here they have the best access to seals, their primary source of food.

As an adaptation to their life on the polar ice cap and its strong reflections from the sun, polar bears' eyes are nearly black. This is typical of both Arctic and Antarctic animals. Their senses of sight and hearing are at least as highly developed as those of humans. Polar bears' noses are so highly evolved that their sense of smell is approximately 100,000 times stronger than that of humans. A polar bear can pick up the scent of a dead seal from a distance of up to 12 miles (20 km).

Over the course of their evolution, polar bears have become almost exclusively carnivorous, and their fur is even thicker than that of brown or black bears. Similar to fiber-optic cables, the translucent hairs conduct light to the black skin beneath the bear's coat, where it is converted into heat. In order to conserve as much heat as possible, polar bears' ears and tails are significantly smaller than those of other bears.

Like all of the large bears, polar bears walk on the entire soles of their feet. Their wide paws distribute

Polar bears normally live as loners. If two young males meet (*above*), they will often engage in playful power struggles which usually increase in intensity. The animals' excellent heat insulation can actually become a problem in fights such as these. Polar bears can easily overheat during long periods of intense exercise; afterwards, they have to lie spread out on the ice to cool off.

the bears' great weight evenly on thin ice, so that it does not break easily. Their broad paws also make it easier for them to swim for hours at a time in the freezing water. They use their front paws like paddles while steering with their hind legs.

Grizzly bears and polar bears are genetically so similar that they can even mate successfully and produce fertile offspring. However, since polar bears and brown bears go into heat at different times, and their habitats are fundamentally different, instances of mating are very rare. In 2006, a very large polar-grizzly hybrid was shot in the Canadian Arctic. Genetic testing revealed that the animal was the first-generation product of a grizzly-polar bear pairing.

can barely detect them. The only thing visible in the picture is the cloud of the polar bear's breath.

Polar bears like to investigate anything that is strange or unfamiliar (*above*). This curiosity is often interpreted as aggressive behavior, but in fact, since they have no natural enemies, they simply see themselves as the unqualified rulers of the Arctic. Their behavior is thus perhaps better defined as

Unlike all the other bear species, polar bears are almost exclusively carnivorous (*right*). Seals make up the largest part of their diet. Nevertheless, only about one in ten of their hunting attempts are successful. Cannibalism is not unusual among adult male polar bears; young bears are frequently killed

BEARS AMONG THEMSELVES

Because of their size, bears require large amounts of food to satisfy their appetites. Their home ranges—one doesn't speak of "territories" in the case of bears—are correspondingly vast. In the barren tundra of the Far North, individual ranges can extend over 200 square miles (500 km²). As a point of comparison, the 5-borough metropolitan area of New York City covers a region of 322 square miles (835 km²). These home ranges are not clearly distinguished from one another, and astonishingly enough, when two bears' areas overlap, they scarcely take notice of one another. Even more unusual is the fact that bears do not emphatically defend their home turf. If food becomes to scarce—for example, if a bear population has grown significantly—and conflicts arise, the bears simply wander on.

In northern Siberia and Alaska as well as in northern Canada, bears will often swim for several miles across shallow waters to islands where vast numbers of seabirds build their nests and raise their young. Perhaps the bears are able to use their excellent sense of smell to sniff out the islands, or perhaps they learned from their mothers that this is a place where they can fatten themselves up in a hurry. The bears remain on the island for as long as it keeps them fed. After all, they are great opportunists.

When the effort to find the last bird's nest becomes too great, the bears finally move on. But not one day sooner, since bears—with the exception of polar bears, who over the course of evolution have developed an energy-saving, almost elegant, ambling pace—lumber along with their legs wide apart, much like overweight human beings, and this costs them a great deal of energy.

Thus, when bears go wandering, they rarely walk cross-country. Instead, wherever possible, they tramp along caribou passes or over ancient trails created by themselves and their kind. These paths, which bears have sunk deep into the ground with their widely-spaced paws, leaving tufts of grass sprouting out of the center stripe, look deceptively like farm tracks created by trucks or tractors.

In their search for food, bears are guided by their excellent memories as well as their exquisitely sensitive noses. They can sniff out gophers deep below the soil or mussels beneath more than a foot of sea mud.

This young Kodiak bear (*below*) is six months old. He first left the winter den with his mother at four months of age.

This female bear (*right*) is quite aloof in her behavior, since she has just given birth for the first time. It will be several days before she tolerates the presence of a human in the vicinity of her only cub.

A bear can catch the scent of another living creature on the wind from a distance of well over half a mile. The scent of a sick or wounded animal can be detected more than a mile away, and carrion as much as three miles away.

A bear's entire world is made up of smells. They store memories of scents the way we humans store visual impressions. Whereas we recognize objects and other people most quickly by their appearance, bears perceive each other as well as other creatures by means of their scent. Voices are also important, but visual images are not. Although bears can only see in black and white, this does not mean that they see poorly, as people frequently assume. On the contrary, bears are often able to discern a human being from a great distance away—even against the wind, so that it would not be able to catch a scent—even though the person could scarcely make out the bear with his or her naked eyes. Animals that can orient themselves very well in twilight or even at night using their senses of smell and hearing do not need to be able to see colors—another indication that bears see in black and white.

Although one occasionally sees photos or animal documentaries of several bears together in one place, this does not mean that a whole family of bears is cavorting together. Such images simply mean that there is a high concentration of food available in that particular area. Thanks to their excellent memories, older bears, in particular, often know the exact day on which they will find food in a particular place—on which bushes the berries will ripen first, at what time and on what river the salmon will be migrating, or in which mountain valleys they can hope to find carcasses, since animals occasionally fall from the steep slopes or are swept down by avalanches in the spring. This also explains why one can see the same bears over and over again in the same places, as if they had a regular appointment calendar. Some of these spots become regular mating areas—for example, a lush meadow of eelgrass where, in mid to late June, when bears go into heat, the first fresh, protein-rich greens lure them in.

Among themselves, bears are not particularly aggressive. In a large meadow full of fresh grass or a wide stretch of tundra where ripe berries are growing, the atmosphere is usually quite calm. The dominant animals take the positions where the most and best food is available, while the lower-ranking bears have to be satisfied with the less-abundant spots. Conflicts are most likely to arise over limited food supplies, for example, a dead moose or caribou, or a river where the salmon are swimming in circles. And of course, when two males compete for a sexually receptive female.

When conflicts do occur, they are usually brief and ferocious, often accompanied by spine-tingling roars. Once dominance or hierarchy has been established, it will not usually be disputed again for some time. This is quite fortunate, since with their powerful fangs and heavy claws, bears can injure each other quite badly.

As already mentioned, however, bears actually prefer to leave each other alone. Unlike wolves or wild boars, they do not live in packs or form family groups. A natural loner, the bear is one of the most antisocial creatures in the animal world. Bears do not even form partnerships of convenience—unless we count the mating relationship, after which the male and female part immediately.

The only lasting social bond in the bear world is that between a mother and her cubs, and that comes to an abrupt end when the mother bear discharges her adolescent offspring into independent life. In reality, this can mean that she brutally drives them away. The young bears are suddenly left to their own devices and are frequently quite unsure of what to do with their new-found freedom. This is the most dangerous phase in a young bear's life. Deprived of their mother's care and protection, not yet completely mature and without a home range of their own, young bears are particularly vulnerable to becoming prey for members of their own species in this transitional period. Siblings can often be observed traveling together years after they have separated from their mother. This sibling attachment and strong orientation to one another dissolves, at the latest, when the young bears reach sexual maturity. Then each animal has to make its way alone.

Brown bears are loners and among the most antisocial

of all mammals. The only social bond that exists

is that between a mother and her cubs.

This is the same young bear pictured on page 50, now three years old. Although he is not yet fully mature, he already has massive paws with long, strong claws. The fur on his head has become strikingly light in color. In the case of young bears, it is very difficult to predict what color their adult coats will ultimately be.

(*Following pages*) A young female grizzly bear attempts to catch salmon. The deeper the water, the slimmer are her chances of success. As playful as this photograph appears, bears expend a great deal of energy on such hunts. Inexperienced or less skilled bears may only catch one fish for every twenty-five attempts.

Some brown bears eat large quantities of particular herbs (*above*) when they are sick as a way of curing themselves. Native Americans traditionally followed unhealthy bears in order to observe them and determine which healing plants they were consuming. They then used the same plants in treating their own illnesses.

Brown bears leave markings on certain trees (*right*), which function as notices for other members of their species. First and foremost, these are symbols of dominance in the bear's home range. The higher a bear can leave its scratch marks or scent on a tree, the higher its position in the hierarchy. By rubbing on these "message trees," particularly with its neck, a bear can also transmit other information, for example, "I'm sick," "I'll be ready

to mate soon," "there are parasites living in and on my body," or "I am an old, weak animal." Bears live in a world made up primarily of scents and smells. It is nearly impossible for us humans to imagine how precisely a bear can perceive its world by means of its sense of smell.

A bear's eyes, like those of nearly all predators, are very small and directed strongly forward (*following pages*). As a hunter, its perception is concentrated in one direction. Prey animals such as deer or rabbits have significantly larger eyes, as well as a larger field of vision, since their eyes are located on the sides of their heads. Bears are often mistakenly thought to be nearsighted. If a bear concentrates precisely on a particular point, it can perceive changes and movement from a great distance away.

56

No two brown bears look alike. Bears have distinctive faces, which can vary enormously. Over the course of many years, I have learned to recognize the majority of animals by their faces. To this end, I photograph the bears I know and any new ones I discover at least once every year—in portrait or half-portrait format if possible. By now, these identifying photos have grown into an extensive collection. I have known some of the bears for twelve years. Their stature and color has sometimes changed greatly, but their facial features remain the same. In the spring, it can be difficult to recognize individual bears since they are sometimes quite emaciated when they emerge from their winter dens, and their fur and claws have grown long.

The same female bear was photographed two months apart (*following pages*). In the left-hand picture, the bear is approximately 90 pounds heavier and completely relaxed. In the picture on the right, her fur is wet and she is extremely tense—she is observing an intruder who wants to hunt for salmon at her favorite fishing spot.

The Aleutian coast of western Alaska (*previous pages*) is littered with driftwood that has been carried in from the entire North Pacific region. The salt-water-bleached wood has often been floating in the ocean for years. The tidal rise—that is, the difference between high and low tide—can be as much as 36 feet (11 m) at the full moon. Twice each day, large areas of tideland lie free of water; bears take advantage of these periods to search for food.

The strong ocean currents bring not only driftwood from the northern Pacific, unfortunately, but the garbage of civilization as well. Bears are aware of this, and some of them regularly search the coastline for flotsam they think they can eat.

White grizzly bears are extremely rare—much more unusual than the white American black bears (Kermode bears) that live in the subarctic rainforests of British Columbia. This white grizzly is not an albino; otherwise, his eyes would be reddish and his nose pink. This four-year-old male is extremely self-confident. In struggles for the dominant position at a feeding area, he even prevails against older members of his species. The First Nations People who live in the region where this bear makes his home honor him like a divine being. Their reverence is so great that some of them even speak about him in whispers.

The play instincts of young bears (*following pages*) are very strong: Everything they do is done playfully. Bear cubs are endlessly curious, and they sometimes wander too far away from their mother during their games or explorations. If they are threatened by other bears, they will usually seek refuge in trees or on outcroppings of rocks. Thanks to their light weight, young brown bears are still good climbers; when they grow older and heavier, this is no longer the case.

Like many other predators, bears are active at night.

They simply sleep whenever they are tired,

and can often be seen napping during the day.

At night (*above*), if bears are illuminated by an artificial light source, their eyes will reflect it. Like other predators, bears see in black and white. Color vision is not important for them, since they perceive the world primarily by means of their noses and ears. Furthermore, since many predators become active only at night, they hunt in a world in which color is not relevant.

Since they are omnivorous, brown bears (*right*) do not have the typical dentition of a predator, which consists solely of incisors and canine teeth (or fangs). Their molars are flattened and have wide, smooth crowns, allowing the bears to chew plant materials as well.

A brown bear's fur (*left*) typically consists of a thick undercoat and a longer topcoat. Seasonal changes are also evident in a bear's coat. The winter coat it acquires for the colder months, for example, is thick and rough, giving it a shaggy appearance. Brown bears' weight is highly dependent on their geographic range, the climate and the availability of food. In all populations, male bears are significantly heavier than females. This female (*right*) has been fishing for several weeks in an abundant salmon stream. She probably weighs well over half a ton.

Bears' weight varies according to the season.

They are at their heaviest in autumn,

just before they retreat to their dens for their winter rest.

In October, the sunlight hours in the Arctic north decrease by about twenty minutes a day. In the evening twilight (*previous pages*)—here in the Bay of Toulik on Alaska's Aleutian Islands— the Kodiak bears appear as silhouettes on the water. When the days grow shorter, bears prepare for their winter rest by putting on fat reserves.

Bear cubs' long period of attachment to their mothers (*above*) and their slow development allow them to precisely observe and copy their mothers' behavior. This is especially important when the young bears begin searching for food on their own. Just as it is for us humans, a sitting position, leaning slightly forward, is quite comfortable for bears (*right*). Very corpulent animals, in particular, will often remain in this position for hours at a time.

Bears have a highly developed sense of orientation. They can find their way back to their home range even when they are released hundreds of miles away.

The romantic atmosphere on Naknek Lake in western Alaska is deceptive. Every year, hundreds of square miles of taiga forest are destroyed by giant brush fires. This is a normal and natural process of regeneration. Well over a hundred miles away from the forest fires, the smoke still hangs in the air, bathing the sun's rays in a dramatic light.

The advanced age of this Kodiak bear (*left*) is evident from his appearance. He could be as much as thirty years old—the maximum life expectancy for brown bears in the wild. In captivity, with the necessary veterinary care and optimum nutrition, brown bears can sometimes live to the age of forty-five. Old bears often suffer from osteoarthritis and can only move very slowly on stiff legs. Other typical characteristics of old age are a mangy-looking coat, bent-down ears, a heavily scarred face (particularly in males)

Uniquely among predators, bears have extremely short tails (*above*). They also lack vibrissae, or whiskers, on their faces. Their most important sense organ is the nose. Bears' eyes are conspicuously small in relation to the size of their heads, and—like those of all predators—their eyes are directed forward, making their field of vision very limited. Their visual acuity is similar to that of human beings. A species-specific feature of the grizzly bear is the muscular hump behind its shoulders, which

THE BEAR FAMILY

Among bears, there is no such thing as a classical family structure; there is only a solo mother with her current litter of cubs. A female bear only becomes ready to mate again when this family has dissolved.

Mating among bears is highly complicated. In the wide-ranging areas in which bears live, it is not always assured that a male bear will be available—and above all, willing—to mate. As a result, females send out early signals that they will soon be in heat by means of a unique scent in their urine. If a male bear picks up this beguiling fragrance, he will remember it and follow it. As soon as he finds the sow that has left the scent, he does not let her out of his sight. He hardly sleeps or eats. He rests when she rests, but always with one eye open. Finally, the day comes when she permits him to mate with her. The first sexual act does not lead to conception; female bears must copulate many times in order to induce ovulation. To make matters even more complicated, the period in which they are able to conceive is very short.

When bears are truly in heat, they mate three to four times a day over a period of several days. A male bear's penis is small in comparison to his body size, but due to a bone in the penis, he does not need to achieve an erection in order to mate. During copula-

tion, the male bites the female in the back of the neck and holds on tightly. Once mating is completed, something very unusual occurs: the fertilized egg cells implant themselves in the mucous membranes of the uterus and lie dormant until autumn. The fate of the egg cells is determined only when the female bear begins her winter rest. If she has not acquired enough fat reserves—which endangers not only her own survival, but also that of her offspring—the egg cells simply die. If she is well-nourished, on the other hand, the egg cells will develop into embryos. The chances that the bear cubs will survive their first winter are then very high.

The average litter size for black bears is two to three cubs; for brown bears and polar bears, it is two. Polar bear mothers with three cubs are very rare, and litters of four are unheard of. Among brown bears as well, a litter of four cubs, like that pictured on the previous pages, is truly the exception.

Strong, watchful and confident females (*below*) will usually not lose any of their cubs during the first three years of their life. It is a part of natural selection, and thus of evolution, that only the strongest animals are able to hold their own and contribute to the continued healthy existence of their species.

Female bears and their cubs (*right*) regularly seek out certain trees where they make scratch marks or rub their fur against the bark in order to leave a message for other bears.

Of all mammals, bears have the smallest newborns in relation to their weight: they are barely the size of a guinea pig. This is less surprising in light of the actual gestation period, which is only about sixty days. When they are born (usually in January), polar and brown bear cubs weigh just over a pound; newborn black bears, born in January and February, weigh even less. All newborn cubs are blind, and their fur is so sparse they appear to be naked. All in all, these are not particularly good preconditions for surviving the coldest part of the year. Until spring arrives—between April and May, depending on the region—the mother bear must nourish her young from her body's reserves; in the coldest regions, this can be half a year. During this time, the female bear consumes no food or water. She remains in her den, nurses her cubs and licks them clean.

Uniquely among mammals, female bears have the ability to convert their cubs' urine—which they lick up to keep their dens clean—into amino acids, that is, protein. Humans would rapidly be poisoned if we were to do the same thing. Scientists have yet to determine what biochemical processes allow bears to do this.

Although female bears give birth to a maximum of four cubs, they have six teats, four on the chest and two on the belly. The latter appear never to be used, evidently because the four upper teats provide much more milk. Each bear cub has its "own" teat, and due to the high fat content of bear milk, the babies gain weight quickly. When they leave their den for the first time, they already weigh between 9 and 13 pounds (4–6 kg). Excursions from the den become progressively longer. In addition to their mother's milk (during the first year, mother bears nurse their cubs an average of four times per day), they begin to consume their first solid food. For polar bears, this is primarily seal. Brown and black bears generally eat grass at first; they may also consume fresh carrion. At the beginning of the summer, their diet is supplemented by salmon that their mother catches for them. If the mother bear has access to good food and is able to produce an abundance of nourishing milk, the young bears will gain weight very quickly. In Alaska and on the Kamchatka Peninsula, young Kodiak bears may weigh up

to 165 to 175 pounds (75–80 kg) near the end of their first year of life.

Young brown bears, who grow and flourish quickly in favorable circumstances, are dismissed from their mother's care after two to three years. In northern Alaska, Canada and Siberia, on the other hand, home of the tundra grizzlies, food is scarce and bears' diets are

primarily vegetarian. Mother bears are not able to produce as much milk, and the winter rest period is extremely long—as much as seven months. Here, young bears may be cared for up to four years. Polar bears also stay with their mothers from two to four years, depending upon the availability of food. Young black bears, however, stay with their mothers for just over a year.

The mortality rate among young bears is very high. Nearly one-third of all cubs do not survive their first year of life. In particular, young bear mothers raising their first litters frequently lose their cubs. Most often, they are killed by male bears.

The height of the bear mating season (*above*) occurs between June and mid-July. If two rival males meet during this time, they will fight over an available female. These fights can be amazingly brutal. Occasionally, one of the opponents may even die as a result of his injuries. Old male bears usually have heavy scars on and around their heads and tattered flews; they may even be missing an ear.

A male bear will often follow and court a female (*right*) for several days before she allows him to copulate with her. Brown bears can afford to have a long mating season, since the eggs cells are not implanted immediately after fertilization. It is not until the beginning of the winter rest period that the physical condition of the female bear's body determines whether the egg cells will develop into embryos or be reabsorbed.

Female bears who lose their cubs early in the year are often ready to mate again within just a few weeks. Bears have even been observed mating in September or October, although the female had been patrolling her home range with her cubs just a short time before.

If good food is abundantly available, young brown bears (*following pages*) can increase their birth weight by a factor of one hundred within the first year of life. The record is held by a young bear from Brooks River, Alaska, who already weighed 125 pounds (57 kg) at the age of ten months.

Like all species of large bears, black bears live a solitary existence, with the exception of females with cubs. Unlike brown bears and polar bears, who raise their offspring for two to four years, young black bears stay with their mothers for just over a year. Consequently, females come into estrus more frequently and are able to raise a larger number of offspring. On average, black bears produce litters of two to three cubs. This female has only one cub, which, thanks to an abundance of food and milk, has grown to above-average size.

Mother bears often seem to handle their first litter of cubs quite carelessly, as if they are not quite mature enough to handle the responsibility. They underestimate dangers and fail to provide sufficient care. This mother, however, is quite the opposite. Her own mother was a very vigilant and self-confident bear, as well. She passed these traits on to her daughter, whose first cub now benefits from them in turn.

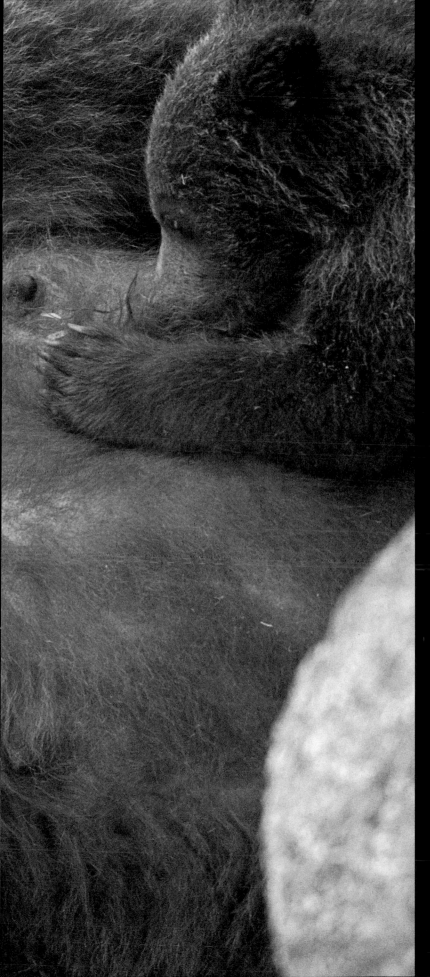

Each cub has its own teat from which it drinks. The highly nourishing milk helps cubs gain weight quickly.

A female brown bear has six teats, four on her chest and two on her belly. The warmth emanating from the teats enables newborn bears to locate the source of milk easily. In the months that follow, the cubs gain more than two pounds a month, and by mid-May, when they emerge from their winter den with their mother, they weigh between 9 and 13 pounds (4–6 kg). Bear milk is characterized by a high protein and fat content (6–17% and 20–40%, respectively).

A mother bear nurses her cubs for at least two years, even though young bears also begin to feed on grasses, berries, herbs, fish and carrion in their first year of life. When the cubs are still small, they nurse for seven to nine minutes up to four times per day. Later, when they are older and stronger, they nurse only twice a day for shorter periods of time.

Young brown bears generally stay with their mother for two and a half years. During the third summer, at the latest, the mother bear weans the cubs and begins to drive them away. Bear mothers' aggressive behavior toward their offspring is most likely triggered by a natural increase in hormone levels. Just a few weeks later, the same female can be seen in the company of a sexually active male.

Play is as important for young bears as it is for human children. Since bears do not live in packs or family groups, social contact between individuals is very limited. The only exception is the relationship between a mother and her cubs. The majority of bears' behavior is innate—that is, they act instinctively. Nevertheless, young brown bears could certainly be characterized as mama's boys and girls: without their mother's care and protection, they would have no chance of survival.

Toward the end of the cub-rearing period, a mother bear is often a nervous wreck. The stresses of nursing for a long period of time, constantly being on the alert for aggressive male intruders, finding sufficient food for herself and her cubs, and teaching the cubs about the world all take their toll on her. At the end of their time together, one can observe that a mother bear distances herself significantly from her young and that her protective instincts are greatly reduced.

Young brown bears are not the least bit afraid of water (*following pages*). Particularly adventurous cubs will accompany their mothers on salmon hunts when they are just over six months old. An ideal fishing lesson goes like this: the mother catches a fish that still has a lot of strength and fight in it; she then passes it on to her cubs, who kill it themselves.

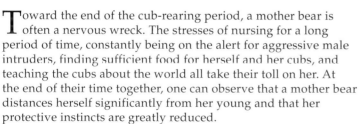

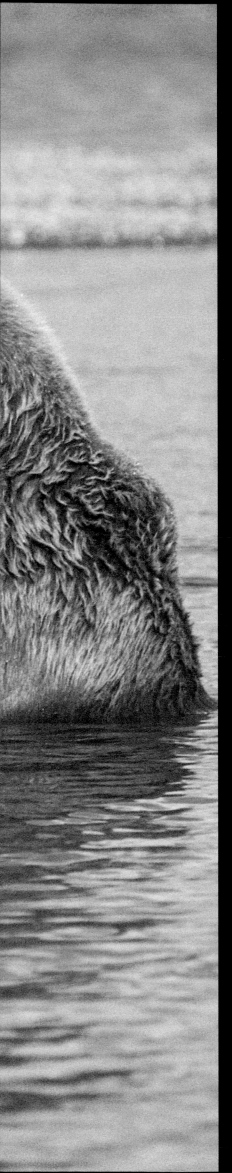

Practice makes perfect:

Mother bears begin teaching their cubs to fish for salmon

when they are just over six months old.

To maintain the strength she needs to raise her cubs and to store enough fat reserves for the winter, a mother bear requires up to 20,000 calories per day. (In comparison, adult women require about 2,000 calories per day.) When they retreat into their dens in the late autumn, a bear's body may consist of up to 50 percent fat. In the weeks before their winter rest begins, bears are pure eating machines. Even though their overall metabolism slows by nearly half during their winter rest, bears nonetheless lose up to 30 percent of their body weight during this period, and females with cubs may lose as much as 40 percent.

Of all the mammals, brown bears and polar bears have the smallest newborns in relation to their body weight. When the cubs are born in the winter den between December and February, they are nearly naked, blind, and about the size of guinea pigs, weighing just over a pound. Since the mother bear does not leave her den during the winter, she produces milk for her cubs from her own fat reserves for a period of several months. In May, when the cubs leave their den for the first time, they have sometimes multiplied their birth weight as much as twenty times. They then immediately begin to consume solid food. From this unusually large litter of four cubs, this mama bear was able to raise three to adulthood. The young bears are the spitting image of their mother.

In their daily life as well, bears regularly take long pauses to rest (*following pages*). This is not true sleep, however, since they maintain a clear awareness of their environment. A bear's period of actual deep sleep lasts only a few minutes a day. It is not a good idea to approach a bear during this time. If it is alarmed, a bear will usually spring into attack position, which can have fatal consequences for human beings.

Young bears take on their mothers' character traits. If the mother is fearful and uncertain, her offspring will learn to be anxious and avoid conflict, as well; while a fierce, confident mother will raise cubs that are strong-willed and fearless.

Approximately 15 percent of all female bears (*above*) continue caring for their young for a third or even a fourth year. Smaller or poorly fed adolescents may stimulate the maternal instinct in their mothers for a longer period.

This white grizzly bear cub (*right and following pages*) looks as if he were covered with snow. With his fluffy coat, he embodies the idea of a cuddly teddy bear. "Frosty," as I called him, was initially afraid of water, but he quickly overcame his fears.

This is a mother polar bear (*above*) with her nearly three-year-old cub. Like brown bears, polar bears have a lower reproductive rate than most mammals. Females produce their first young at the age of four to six years. And since the young bears stay with their mothers for approximately thirty months, three years usually elapse between successive litters. Thus, with a life expectancy of about twenty years, a female bear gives birth only four to six times in her lifetime.

Polar bears roam about frequently (*above right and below*) and often cover truly enormous distances. During its lifetime, the average polar bear may traverse more than 100,000 square miles (260,000 km²) of the Arctic wilderness. Polar bears move at an average speed of about 2.5 miles (4 km) per hour, but when they find it necessary they can run at speeds up to 28 miles (45 km) per

hour. They tend to be most active when the temperature is between −4 and +5 °F. Their broad paws allow them to walk across even deep snow without sinking in, as if they were wearing snowshoes. In northern Alaska, a polar bear was once observed wandering inland along a frozen riverbed for more than 55 miles (90 km).

This young mother bear's play instinct (*following pages*) was still very strong. The sow took advantage of every opportunity to tumble and play with her cub. Since this was her first and only offspring, the cub had no siblings to play with. Nevertheless, it instinctively used every possibility it could to learn about life. Bear cubs' play not only trains their muscles and endurance, it also teaches them about dominance, hierarchy, assertiveness and self-confidence.

Since bears live solitary lives, and close relationships exist only between mothers and their cubs, it is not necessary for them to communicate beyond the most basic messages. Bears have neither a highly expressive body language nor a complex repertoire of sounds. Their facial muscles do not allow for any expression, their ears are relatively small, and their stub tails are not suitable for sending signals.

Mother bears always drive their offspring away in the springtime.

Before they go their separate ways, the mother and her cubs

spend a final winter rest period together.

Scarcity of food is the primary reason that bears take a rest period in the winter. As the dark and cold season approaches, less nutritious food is readily available. Then it will not be long before the bear family retreats into its winter den. The better fed the cubs and their mother are at the beginning of the inactive period, the greater their chances of surviving the winter in good health.

Three seconds before flight: this female and one of her cubs have spotted a male bear that looks threatening. Unlike wolves or lions, bears are not highly communicative and can only make a few different sounds. By clapping their jaws and exhaling percussively, they signal danger and extreme excitement to those around them. These warning sounds can also be heard when people enter a bear's personal space or intrude on a bear family.

Anyone who has spent the summer months in the northern latitudes (*following pages*) will have distinct memories of the vast legions of mosquitoes that exist there. Nearly all the animals of the North are plagued by these pests, even though they are extremely important for the ecosystem. Mosquito larvae, in particular, constitute the primary diet of many species of fish and birds. Thanks to their thick, matted fur, young bears are fairly well protected from mosquito bites; only their sensitive noses are vulnerable.

These photos were taken along the Aleutian coastline. The driftwood that has been carried far inland marks the flood line of the stormy ocean during the winter months. The sea grass growing on the offshore meadows is very high in protein; it forms an excellent basis for the bears' diet. Since plants are more complex to digest than meat, bears' stomachs are larger in proportion to their body size than those of wolves or lions. Specialized predators constantly live between the extremes of abundance and famine. Since bears' diets are incredibly diverse, this does not happen to them. During the summer months, nearly every region of the North contains a wealth of edible green plants.

BEAR VERSUS BEAR:
BATTLE OF THE GIANTS

like all other young animals, cubs like to romp about and spar with their siblings and their mother. In adolescent bears, these scuffles are still playful in nature; the youngsters are testing their limits and preparing for their life in the wild. Serious fights can be observed only among fully mature bears.

Fights between adult bears are relatively rare. One reason for this is the fact that bears live in very large home areas. These areas can overlap—in contrast to the territories of many other animals, which are generally clearly marked and delineated. However, the sheer size of their home range—around 75 square miles (200 km^2) in regions where many brown bears live, and up to 200 square miles (500 km^2) in the barren, sparsely populated Far North—means that bears seldom cross each other's paths. Secondly, bears are loners. Battles over hierarchy within a clan or pack do not exist. This lifestyle already ensures that bears are relatively relaxed and easy-going creatures who are more likely to resolve conflicts through posturing and bravado than through actual physical force.

This scenario changes abruptly, though, when conflicts arise over the best feeding spot, the first available food of the year or a sexually receptive female. Then the battle of the giants begins, in which the fundamental issue is always the same: establishment of dominance and hierarchy. Bears vary widely as far as their basic personalities are concerned. There are very aggressive animals and timid ones; some are incredibly curious and others reserved. Depending upon how they were influenced by their mothers, some bears prefer to avoid conflict, while others are always ready for a fight. Among females as well, there are certainly those whose behavior signalizes dominance and will even enter into conflicts with large males. Here, the dispute is nearly always over the best source of food, be it an animal carcass, a fishing hole or a spot where mussels or ripe berries can be found in abundance. After all, a female bear must ensure that not only she, but also her offspring, are well fed before they enter their winter dens. Not surprisingly, fights between females can be observed most frequently in the autumn.

When a dominant bear approaches a good feeding spot, other bears will often retreat without a fight. But if two equally strong, self-confident and, above all, determined bears come face to face, a fight will

What looks like an out-and-out altercation here is simply playful jockeying for strength and position. These two young males are not yet sexually mature. Nevertheless, this youthful training for future battles is an important part of their preparation for life as adult bears.

inevitably ensue. This is true whether the animals involved are male or female, although a mother is always higher in status than a female without cubs. These battles are often waged with enormous vehemence and determination—and in the case of large males can even lead to the death of one of the opponents. This seldom occurs with females, although they may certainly sustain injuries. If one male bear kills another in a fight, he will eat all or part of the carcass. Such behavior is not unusual for predators, but it is particularly common among bears.

Although many fights occur during mating season, the primary conflict is not necessarily over reproduction, but rather access to food. Since in some regions the mating season coincides with the first appearance of lush sea grasses, many bears may gather in these feeding areas and compete for the best spots—by force, if necessary.

It is remarkable among bears that even weaker males who tend to avoid conflicts or who may have lost a fight can still be quite successful with the opposite sex. In fact, young females usually prefer more youthful, weaker males, since they have learned from their mothers that the more dangerous older bulls are likely to attack their cubs. There are several reasons for this behavior: to ensure the survival of the strongest offspring; to regulate the population in the absence of any natural enemies; as well as the fact that when a female loses her young, she will enter estrus again very soon afterwards—often in the same year. However, this does not mean that a sow will mate with the same male bear who killed her last litter, no matter how persistently he may pursue her.

If two males do engage in a serious fight, they may carry it out to the utmost extreme, a situation that I have personally witnessed. In this case, one of the combatants was the "Lord of the Valley," an extremely large and heavy bear between twenty-five and thirty years of age and weighing nearly two tons, who normally lived a secluded life. When a similarly massive but significantly younger male (between fifteen and twenty years old) appeared, the two bears clashed violently and entered into a fight that lasted several

hours. There were occasional pauses, but the conflict was repeatedly rekindled by the two opponents' aggression and drive for dominance. The turmoil of their fight could be heard from far away. The next day, the site of their conflict looked like a battlefield: across an area of approximately 30 by 30 yards, the soil had been churned up, trees had been uprooted

and broken branches were strewn everywhere. The younger bear had sustained severe bite wounds; the older male had paid for the fight with his life. The victor ate part of his opponent's carcass; he then attempted to bury the rest in order to safeguard his prize. Cannibalism is not unusual among bears. Over the next few days, several older males approached the carcass and consumed parts of it. The salmon in the nearby river were no longer of any interest to them. Since bear flesh is highly nutritious, members of the same species will eat it readily. Nevertheless, bears do not regard each other as prey. If one bear is killed by another, there is always a reason for it beyond simply for food.

This playful conflict gradually became serious. In the course of their practice session for later life, the two young males became so excited that their behavior became increasingly aggressive. After more than half an hour of violent biting, the two youngsters suddenly broke apart and desisted. Both were injured, and because of their excellent insulation, their bodies were overheated. Following separate paths, they both headed for the nearby water and cooled themselves off for an extended period.

Fights between two male bears

are rarely pursued to

the furthest extreme.

Even at times when food is abundant, conflicts between bears are a regular occurrence. Ultimately, the dispute is not only over the quarry itself, but over precedence at the best hunting or foraging areas.

Among bears, similarly to other predators, an animal's size and aggressiveness determine his or her position in the hierarchy. In most cases, a bear's body language, along with a few vocal utterances, are sufficient to clarify the situation. This is true not only for the dominant animal, but for its subordinate opponents as well.

Females with cubs rank just below mature males in the hierarchy. Their frequently aggressive behavior allows them to prevail even over stronger bears. Here, although the dark brown female has a physical advantage over the mother with her nearly three-year-old offspring, the mother has a higher status. Since the dark brown female is pregnant, she needs to put on a great deal of weight to provide for herself and her unborn young during the winter, so she persistently attempts to take over the fishing area.

147

A serious fight can go on for several hours, interspersed with pauses, but repeatedly rekindled by the bears' desire for dominance.

The death rate among adult brown bears (*right*) is low, at less than 5 percent. For young animals, the situation is quite different. In areas where the concentration of bears is high, there is much stronger competition among the animals. Approximately one-third of all cubs do not survive their first year. Another 15 to 20 percent perish in the second year of life, and 25 to 30 percent of young animals whose mothers release them into independent life do not reach sexual maturity. The primary causes of death are other bears or the consequences of undernourishment.

In fights between adult males (*following pages*), severe or fatal injuries are the exception rather than the rule. Only rarely do bears aspire to fight to the death. In most cases, one of the combatants will give up and flee to safety after just a few minutes.

ON THE HUNT

Its strength, skill, speed and self-confidence make the grizzly bear an excellent hunter. Thanks to its powerful paws, it is capable of overpowering almost any other animal. The fact that bears have evolved into omnivores is a testament to a general problem that exists among predators. The animals on which they prey are often difficult to catch or only available in large numbers at certain times of the year. Predators thus constantly cycle between periods of abundance and times of famine. When they make a catch, they may consume up to one-fifth of their own body weight at a single meal, since it may be a long time until the next successful hunt.

As far as their diet is concerned, bears tend to adapt to the region in which they live. In the tundras of Alaska, Canada and Siberia or the impassable terrain of the Himalayas, where prey is scarce, bears often satisfy most of their need for animal protein and fat by catching gophers. They may occasionally plunder a bird's nest for eggs, or if they are extremely lucky, they can feast on a dead animal such as a dall sheep or a caribou. Otherwise, their diet is vegetarian. There are even some bears who feed primarily on grass and nevertheless grow to an impressive size.

In general, a bear's size and condition are strongly dependent upon its diet. The grizzly bears of Kodiak

Island in southwestern Alaska—also called Kodiak bears—and the bears of the Kamchatka Peninsula bordering on Siberia are the largest brown bears in the world. Not surprisingly, these enormous bears—collectively called coastal brown bears—have nearly year-round access to food that is rich in protein: fish, particularly salmon, which they catch during the annual migration of the fish to their spawning grounds; sea grass, which provides lots of fat, protein and minerals; as well as mussels, which bears dig out of the mud at ebb tide after locating them precisely with their highly sensitive noses. Bears may also seek out stranded animals along the coast, such as whales, sea lions or seals. The carcass of a single beached humpback whale can feed thirty bears or more for several months.

This hearty menu ensures that the gigantic bears of Kodiak and Kamchatka can enter their winter dens at weights of up to one ton. And since the winter rest period in these temperate climates is barely two months long—even shorter in mild winters—bears do

Northern Canada and Alaska are carpeted and crisscrossed with countless bodies of water. During the primary salmon migration period, bears are drawn to the best fishing grounds as if by magic.

not lose as much weight during that time as in other regions. In central Alaska, for example, the winter rest period lasts for six months or longer, and bears are emaciated when they emerge from their dens.

Due to the combination of a more meager diet, a harsher climate, and a significantly longer winter rest period in the tundra or in high mountains, bears in these regions are substantially smaller and lighter. It makes an enormous difference whether a bear has to dig laboriously for roots every day and nourish itself with small berries, grass that is not especially nutritious and the occasional gopher or whether it has access to an abundant supply of substantial food—and whether it has to live off of its winter reserves for six months or only two.

Regardless of the region in which they live and the foods they indulge in throughout the year, bears develop a craving for certain plant foods shortly before their winter denning period begins. For example, they eat rose hips as well as wilted grass, withered mosses and lichens. This dry, high-fiber food helps the animals to excrete waste before their winter rest. Some bears travel over tremendous distances in search of food. Older bears, for instance, know exactly in which rivers the first salmon of the year will appear and in which direction they will migrate next. Some of this knowledge was passed on to them by their mothers, while other information is gathered through their own experience.

Other bears systematically seek out hillsides that are covered with willows and alder bushes every spring, since they know that female moose hide their calves there. The young moose are left alone during the day—the mother returns only to nurse—making them an easy prey for bears. Caribou calves are similarly easy to catch. Their mothers do not leave them alone the way moose cows do; they are forced to keep up with the herd immediately after birth. A calf that is too weak or too slow, however, quickly becomes fodder for predators.

Despite their stature and strength, bears seldom dare to attack an adult moose; the danger of incurring serious injury from its antlers or its sharp-edged hooves is too great. After all, a mature bull moose can weigh up to 1,650 pounds (750 kg) and a cow up to 1,300 (600 kg). Faced with an animal of this magnitude, even a bear is somewhat out of its league. Furthermore, moose can move very fast. Bears are excellent sprinters—they can run as fast as 40 miles (65 km) per hour for short distances, equivalent in speed to a racehorse—but they cannot maintain this rate for very long. Therefore, grizzlies have to stalk and draw extremely close to fast-moving flight animals before they attack.

Mature, healthy male moose have nothing to fear from grizzly bears, since they are too well-equipped to defend themselves to come into question as potential prey. Nevertheless, during the mating season, a bull moose might be seriously injured by an antler goring from a rival; then he could certainly fall victim to bears or wolves. I once witnessed a female grizzly bear killing a mature cow moose. The bear sow had three yearling cubs and lived in a region without any significant fishing grounds. A few weeks previously, the moose had lost her calf to a bear attack. Now she had unwittingly wandered in the direction of the lurking mother bear with the wind at her back. The bear launched her attack from close range. At a weight of around 1,300 pounds (600 kg), the cow was not capable of fleeing fast enough, but she defended herself with her dangerous hooves. The battle between the two animals continued for over an hour, until the female grizzly was finally able to grasp the moose high on the throat and pull her to the ground. For nearly three weeks, the moose carcass provided food for the family of bears, countless ravens, Arctic foxes and a single wolf.

Other animals are difficult targets for bears for a variety of reasons. Dall sheep, for example, live in extremely craggy terrain that is nearly inaccessible, and they are excellent climbers, quick and alert. Musk oxen have a different strategy: they move into a type of corral formation in which the stronger animals form a circle around the smaller and weaker members of the group and turn their impressively horned heads toward their attacker.

At Brooks Falls, a big fat catch practically jumps into the bears' mouths in the form of salmon. All they need to do is wait patiently, and their stomachs will be filled with protein-rich sustenance.

Some bears can hardly wait for the salmon to reach the rapids of Brooks Falls in Alaska. The salmon migration takes place in exactly the same spot every year, and the time varies by only a few days. From experience, bears know where the best fishing spots are, and judging from the length of the daylight hours, they can predict the days on which the fish will arrive.

When the first sockeye salmon arrive at Alaska's Brooks Falls (*previous pages*), their color is still entirely silver. Only after spending several weeks in fresh water do their bodies turn red and their heads green. In one Native American language, the word for sockeye salmon is something like "the jumper"—and they certainly do justice to that title. Only the strongest fish can surmount this waterfall. The cold, oxygen-rich streams and rivers provide ideal mating conditions for the salmon. These fish mate only in the same location where they themselves hatched several years before. Their extraordinary sense of smell leads them to within feet of the exact spot where they were born.

The more plentiful the salmon that swim up the river, the more brown bears gather at the falls. The best fishing spots, naturally, are claimed by the highest-ranking bears. Bears lower on the hierarchy—particularly young males and females without cubs— have to try their luck fishing in the eddies. Many salmon misjudge the distance when they attempt to jump over the waterfall, and instead of landing in the calm water on the other side of the cascade, fall back into the maelstrom. The result is that thousands of salmon can become trapped underneath the waterfall. At the height of the migration season, particularly skillful bears can retrieve as many as fifty fish from the water each day.

For the bears of this region, Brooks Falls is a location where their most gluttonous dreams come true. Many animals have developed their own personal fishing techniques with which they are very successful. At the beginning of the salmon season, bears will generally eat entire fish, but they become increasingly selective as time goes on. They will often let male salmon fall back into the water. Their flesh is not as rich as that of the females, and their milk (sperm) contains little fat or nutrients. During the most abundant fishing periods, bears consume only the extremely fatty caviar, the brain, and the skin of the female salmon. The rest of the fish is left for the seagulls—or for younger bears, who are already waiting downstream for the carcasses to reach them.

Moose cows frequently deposit their newborn calves in dense scrubland. In the first few weeks of life, young moose do not give off any scent and are therefore difficult for predators to locate. The mother returns only twice each day to nurse her calf. If a cow moose is taken by surprise in such a situation, she may react very aggressively and use her sharp-edged hooves to attack even large predators such as bears, wolves or wolverines. As the unqualified rulers of the north, bears are well aware of their limitations. Large, healthy animals such as bull moose—who are also equipped with sharp antlers—are treated with respect. Nevertheless, a bear will always check to see if an animal may be injured, which might make a successful attack a possibility.

Caribou, baby musk ox, dall sheep, moose calf, groundhog,

bird eggs, salmon or mussels, herbs, grasses or berries:

bears are generalists to whom everything tastes good.

Grizzly bears will prey on musk oxen (*top left*) only seldom. Dall sheep (*top right*) live primarily on very craggy terrain, making these extraordinary climbers virtually inaccessible to grizzlies. Only when they cross a valley can they become an easy target for bears and wolves. Caribou calves (*bottom left*) have to travel with their herd immediately after they are born. Wolves or grizzly bears will often follow caribou herds in order to seize any sick or weak young animals. The Arctic ground squirrel (*bottom right*) is an important source of food only for the tundra grizzlies of the Far North. Since these rodents are true hibernators, they store enormous fat deposits in their bodies. Bears will regularly dig the little rodents out from their winter dens.

A female grizzly bear (*above*) who just recently emerged from her winter rest has caught a newborn moose calf. Beginning in mid-May, experienced bears will systematically seek out the traditional birthplaces of the moose. In regions that have a high concentration of bears and wolves, up to 80 percent of all young moose may be killed in this way in a given year.

Bears and wolves, both excellent hunters, are at the very top of the food chain. Wolves are purely carnivorous and seldom compete directly with bears for food. They rarely live alone, but rather in packs—and they are constantly on the hunt. The two species generally avoid one another, and confrontations occur only seldom. On the other hand, wolves know that if a grizzly bear has killed a large animal, there will usually be something left over for them. In these photos, however, the bear's catch is small and she has claimed it for herself. The female grizzly, who is wearing a tracking collar, has captured a caribou calf. It weighs only about 35 pounds (15 kg), and she will consume it within a few minutes. The wolf's strategy is to provoke the bear into attacking and chasing him so that he can circle back to the dead calf and escape with the catch. All of his attempts were unsuccessful, however, and the bear did not leave a single morsel of the caribou calf behind.

When Mount Katmai in southwestern Alaska (*previous pages*) erupted on June 6, 1912, it expelled enormous quantities of volcanic ash and lava into the atmosphere. An area of a hundred square miles or more was carpeted with a thick layer of ash, and all life forms seemed to have been extinguished for ages to come. The rivers and streams were so clogged with ash that it was impossible for the salmon to move forward. But the region's heavy precipitation and mild climate helped vegetation grow back again during the decades that followed, and even the salmon gradually returned to mate in its waters.

During the peak season (*left*), up to ten bears may share the rich fishing grounds at Brooks Falls at the same time. The exposure time for this photo was one and a half seconds. Since there was never a moment when all of the bears were standing perfectly still, the slow shutter speed makes them appear slightly blurred. During the most abundant period, some young bears can satisfy themselves very well without great exertion (*right*) by feeding on the higher-ranking animals' leftovers.

Bears' feeding habits are first and foremost geared toward gaining weight. During peak periods, adult animals can gain up to 4.5 pounds (2 kg) per day.

The water has not yet completely drained from the fjords at low tide (*following pages*), but the first hungry bears have already ventured into the tidal flats in search of mussels.

Along the northern Canadian and Alaskan coastlines, giant Kodiak bears dig for mussels in the mudflats. Thanks to the tides, the shellfish are available throughout the year. Bears prefer food sources such as these, which are constantly replenished. Although the mussels may not appear to be particularly abundant or accessible at first glance, they are a reliable basis for the bears' diet.

Hard-shelled scallops (*following pages*) are extremely high in fat and protein. After digging them up, bears skillfully open the shells with their claws. Young bears who have not yet mastered this technique simply bite through the scallops, suck out the contents and spit the shells back out.

Mussels are a delicacy for bears, rich in fat and protein. Bears frequently wander through the mudflats at ebb tide, using their sensitive noses to seek out the perfect location to dig for the tasty shellfish.

On Kodiak Island (*previous pages*), even strong male bears travel to the tidal flats to search for mussels after their winter rest period. Here, two large males dug for mussels at the same time without ever coming into conflict.

Approximately twenty-five different Kodiak bears regularly fed on the remains of this beached humpback whale. The whale apparently became stranded on the Aleutian coast during a winter storm. The smell of the carcass was perceptible from more than a quarter mile away. Even though the whale meat could hardly have been very appetizing for the bears at this point, there was a clear feeding hierarchy. Only after the older males had eaten their fill for three days were the younger animals allowed to approach the carcass. There were no female bears with cubs present. The mood among the animals at this feeding ground was unusually nervous, irritable and aggressive.

A whale carcass is a true windfall. With its high fat content,

the meat can keep them well fed for several weeks.

Bears from all across the region are magically attracted by the scent.

Buoys and floaters torn from fishing nets often turn up in the drift line along the coastal areas of the Aleutian Islands. In the past, these objects were made of glass, cork, wood or metal; nowadays they are almost always made from rubber or plastic. Bears find their scent and consistency irresistible. They will bite, chew on or drag the items around with them for hours at a time.

In some years, the great salmon migrations do not take place in certain rivers and streams (*previous pages*). This is in part due to the fact that Pacific species of salmon are highly sensitive to changing climactic conditions, such as ever-warmer global temperatures, which have also led to the warming of the oceans and the displacement or disruption of ocean currents. In addition, the number of fish that take part in migration is not the same from one year to the next. In years of heavy migration, a large number of the fish will spawn, as well. Then, depending upon the species, it may take between three and seven years for those salmon to return to their birthplace. Thus, there can be large periodic variations in the amount of food that is available to bears.

For the grizzly bears that live far out on the Aleutian Islands, large, gnarled pieces of driftwood such as these provide their only opportunity to test their climbing abilities on real wood. The region's harsh climate and many storms prevent any trees from growing here. Almost every bear that encounters one of these picturesque logs seems compelled to leave its calling card behind. The tree trunks function simultaneously as sports equipment and message centers.

Juicy herbs and grasses are an important element of a bear's diet.

Herbs also help to cleanse the intestines before their winter rest

and ease the symptoms of certain illnesses.

Approximately 20 to 30 million years ago, the ancestors of today's large bears were typical carnivores, about the size of foxes. Over the course of evolution, however, the features that allowed the animals to consume a greater proportion of vegetarian food in their diet became more pronounced. In contrast to specialized predators such as wolves, bears have large molars with flattened, uneven surfaces that are ideally suited for grinding up grasses and roots.

Even in the area of vegetarian cuisine, bears are true gourmets. In meadows filled with herbs and flowers, observers have repeatedly noted that bears consume only certain types of shrubs, flowers or plants, and that they were willing to travel long distances in order to find them. They graze most intensively in sea grass meadows where the plants are particularly rich in protein and minerals. Some grizzlies are connoisseurs of willow roots. The root bark, in particular, is highly nutritious and contains the ingredient acetylsalicylic acid—in other words, aspirin. Native American shamans have long been aware of this, and also used these roots to prepare medicines for treating pain and fever.

Bears can consume approximately 20,000 calories per day—the equivalent of about thirty large servings of spaghetti. When the major salmon migrations come to an end, there are no remaining significant food sources available for most Kodiak bears. The remainder of their diet prior to the winter rest period often consists of berries. The sugar content provides bears with additional energy, and the high percentage of fiber in the berries serves as a cleansing agent for the bears' digestive system, as do certain herbs. Wild rose hips contain a large dose of vitamin C and provide a particularly good cleansing for bears' intestines.

In the northernmost areas of their geographic range,

brown bears spend about 60 percent of their life span in a state of deep sleep.

Scarcity of food is the primary reason for their winter rest period.

In late autumn, before winter sets in with full force, brown bears retreat into their dens for their winter rest. They enter their caves at varying points in time depending on their gender, family status and age. Pregnant females and mothers with cubs make up the advance party, and the last to retreat are the dominant males. Each bear digs out their own den, which is usually remarkably small. It consists of a short tunnel—approximately 3 feet (1 m) long—and a chamber that provides just enough space for the bear or bears in question. Many of these dens collapse in the springtime when the soil thaws out. Young bears who are not well nourished before the winter denning begins have only a very slim chance of surviving their long winter sleep.

It won't be long until this old male bear (*following pages*) also retreats into his winter den, and he will be one of the last to do so. At nearly 40 years of age, he is one of the oldest living brown bears recorded in the wild. The bodies or skeletons of old bears who have perished are almost never found. Very old, sick or weak animals are often eaten by other members of their species—or they simply die in their winter dens and never reemerge.

BEARS AND HUMANS

In myths and fairy tales, the bear is always the wise, clever character who provides solutions, never an evil figure. A bear is the embodiment of strength, aloof and independent—exactly the same image that bears still have today in regions where people live in, with and from the natural world. In North America, for example, ever since the time when humans still lived as hunters and gatherers—and, with their primitive weapons, were powerless against bears—the bear has been regarded as an almost godlike, invincible creature. In myths and natural theology, as well as on the totem poles of First Nations Peoples, the bear—along with the wolf—occupies a place at the top. People did not fight bears, but instead attempted to integrate them into the clan or family in order to take part in their strength.

In Eastern Europe and the vast regions of Siberia, bears represent shrewdness, wisdom and superiority, but also conquest—we need only think of the expression "the realm of the Russian bear." In Asia, thanks to bears' strength and aura, parts of their bodies have been sought-after aphrodisiacs since time immemorial. The flesh of their paws and their gall bladders are thought to have magical powers. In traditional Chinese medicine, bear bile is also believed to have a variety of healing effects.

A cult of the bear once existed in Europe as well, as can be seen from prehistoric cave paintings and sculptures made of ivory and bone. Here, too, the bear was a symbol of strength, virility and intelligence—at least until it came into conflict with human culture. Particularly in Central Europe—where people settled down and began cultivating the land and raising livestock quite early and which was relatively densely populated even several centuries ago—bears quickly became the declared enemies of humanity. They took full advantage of the riches of civilization, feeding on grain from the fields, plundering beehives, stealing fruit from orchards, and killing sheep, pigs and cattle. Consequently, bears were persecuted and their populations decimated to the point that in wide-ranging areas, they live on only in legends and fairy tales.

More than ten years ago I became the first cameraman in the world who was able to film a wild grizzly bear under water (*below*). It took about two months for the bear to become accustomed to my proximity and allow me to come within just a few feet of him under water. On land (*right*), he was practically indifferent to my presence, but as soon as I entered the ice-cold water with my diving suit on, that trust disappeared. Apparently, a two-legged creature approaching him underwater did not fit in the bear's perception of reality. Nevertheless, the bear never tried to attack me; rather, he always attempted to evade me.

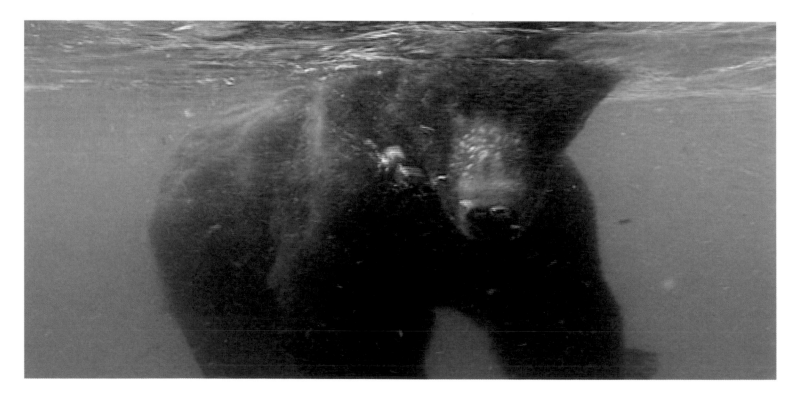

Today, particularly in the regions where bears no longer live in the wild, people have an extremely contradictory image of the animals. On the one hand, there is the beloved Teddy bear, the furry, cuddly stuffed toy that shares our childhood beds—or the baby polar bear Knut, who attracted a torrent of visitors from all over the world to the Berlin Zoo. With their furry appearance and lumbering gait, even mature bears radiate "cuteness." Perhaps more than any other adult creature, they exemplify Konrad Lorenz's concept of *Kindchenschema*—a set of childlike characteristics that stimulate tender emotions and nurturing instincts. On the other hand, bears are dangerous predators that—like the brown bear Bruno who made news in Germany in 2006—invade our front yards and stir up irrational fears. Only a few people saw Bruno, the first wild brown bear to appear in Germany in over 170 years, as a symbol of the resurgence of an intact balance of nature. Bears are tolerated as cuddly toys or circus attractions, but nobody wants to see them running free in the wild.

Bruno offered people a chance to provide brown bears with a native home in Germany once again. Instead of killing him, observers could have fitted him with a sensor and let his activities be monitored by biologists or forest rangers. Fireworks or rubber bullets could have been used to keep him away from human settlements and individual farms. The bear would quickly have learned to avoid close contact with human beings. This approach works well in North America—so much so that even "problem bears" need to be destroyed only in truly exceptional cases.

In other parts of the world, human beings have learned to live in close proximity with bears, and thanks to their adaptability and intelligence, bears have learned to make the most of the situation. Since bears do not like to walk—particularly not over any great distance—they tend to use paths created by people, be they farm tracks or gravel roads. In some areas, bears specialize in human garbage as a source of food, and they are able to live quite well from it. Studies conducted in Romania show that such bears produce more offspring than their relatives in the wilds of the Carpathian Mountains, who feed on carrion, small animals and plants. What the long-term effects of this wonderful garbage recycling system might be, however, is a different issue.

The most common mistake people make when dealing with bears is that of basing their interpretations of bears' behavior and feelings, thoughts and way of life on their own ways of thinking and feeling. Human beings, however, are social and emotional creatures who live together in communities. All of these characteristics are foreign to bears. Therefore, it would make more sense for humans to ask themselves such questions as: How does this bear see me? What does he see in me at the moment that he is excited or afraid, when he claps his jaw or assumes an aggressive pose? Does he see me as an enemy, an intruder into his territory, as a danger? In order to make such judgments—and above all, to react appropriately—you need a lot of experience and very strong nerves.

Nevertheless, even in regions where the bear population is relatively high, attacks on human beings are rare. The cases in which people have been attacked—and in the worst cases, even killed—by bears, are usually exceptional situations. Almost all of the conflicts that have occurred between humans and bears in the last twenty years—with very few exceptions—were provoked by mistakes on the part of the people involved. They surprised a bear while it was sleeping and overstepped its personal boundaries, or the person was wearing or carrying a perfume—a tube of lip balm in a jacket pocket, a tube of toothpaste in the tent, or sunscreen or cologne on their skin. Since bears are led by their noses, they want to investigate any interesting scent, and if necessary, they will incapacitate a human being with a blow of their paws or a bite in the neck in order to do so. In another case, a person may have tried to drive away a bear that was rummaging through a pile of garbage, attacking livestock or had made its way into a building. From the bear's point of view, someone wanted to compete for its prey or feeding area, and it needed to defend it.

In Europe, bear populations are slowly beginning to increase again. Wildlife preserves and migration

Since brown bear populations are increasing in the Alpine region,

the animals will soon need to expand into new areas.

corridors are being created in order to once again provide the large predators with a basis for existence. These projects have enjoyed great success in North America and Scandinavia as well as in Eastern Europe. In general, it seems that in countries where brown bears have never been completely exterminated, the people—and ultimately, the politicians—react more constructively and search for appropriate solutions for coexisting with these large predators.

With the exception of primates (*above and following pages*), there are no other mammals that can adopt poses so similar to those of humans. At moments such as these, bears also look like overgrown teddy bears. This is one of the many reasons why people find bears so appealing.

Bears are led by their noses, and they will follow

the tantalizing smells of human civilization. In many areas

of North America, bears have learned to live side by side with human beings.

In all of North America (*previous pages*), an average of six people are killed by brown bears each year. During the same time period, several thousand people are killed in traffic accidents. The few accidental deaths involving brown bears can usually be traced to an error on the part of the person involved—for example, when a human being and a bear find themselves standing face to face without warning. The surprised animal will then attack in order to defend itself, its prey or its young. As a general rule, however, bears are shy and will avoid encounters with people if the people make their presence known in an area where bears live.

So-called problem bears can be found everywhere in North America in areas where people have settled close to a wilderness region and bears are able to feed themselves partially from the garbage of civilization. Unlike the case of Bruno in Germany, however, such bears are not destroyed immediately; rather, people attempt to recondition them. Through the use of rubber bullets, fireworks or tear gas, bears learn to equate close proximity to human settlements with pain, fear and stress. Since bears are highly intelligent, they grasp these lessons very quickly and retain what they have learned.

The Trans-Alaska Pipeline is the lifeline of the largest state in the USA. For over thirty years now, approximately $800 (US) worth of crude oil have flowed through this system every second. The pipeline was a masterwork of engineering technology: built on top of the permafrost, it is earthquake-proof and able to withstand extreme temperature variations of over 200 °F (100 °C). The pipeline snakes its way 800 miles (1300 km) from Prudhoe Bay in the north to the ice-free port of Valdez on Prince William Sound in the south. The animals of the Far North have come to accept these monstrous foreign objects and now scarcely pay any attention to them.

A welcome photo opportunity: In some areas, people's presence doesn't seem to disturb brown bears in the least. Caution is advised nonetheless, since bears can also react completely unpredictably.

AREA CLOSED

Entering a closed area or removal of this sign is punishable by a fine of up to $500 or imprisonment for 6 months, or both.

BEAR DANGER

DENALI NATIONAL PARK AND PRESERVE, ALASKA

The national parks of the United States and Canada maintain certain rules regarding humans' interactions with nature. If the park administration learns that a bear has caught a large animal, people will be barred from a wide area surrounding the catch site. The danger is too great that the bear will feel its catch is threatened by the presence of people and react aggressively. In Denali National Park in Alaska (*left*), bears have become accustomed to bus traffic. Since the bears always have the right of way, long lines of buses sometimes get backed up. Every visitor wants to have a chance to take a photo of a bear from a safe vantage point.

Alaska and northern Canada (*previous pages*) are dream destinations for fishermen. Nowadays, thanks to seaplanes, sport anglers can reach even the most remote fishing areas—but they are seldom alone when they get there. Wherever lots of fish are jumping, there will be bears, too. On Alaska's Brooks River, some female bears have become highly skilled at stealing fish right off of anglers' hooks; after all, a fish on a hook is an easier catch. Even before the salmon or rainbow trout land in the dip net, the bears have grabbed them, torn off the line and gobbled them down right before the outraged fishermen's astonished eyes. Once a fish is on the hook, some bear sows can even tell from the creaking sounds of the fishing reel whether the salmon on the end is large or small.

On clear nights (*left*), a breathtakingly beautiful display of light can be seen in the starry northern sky. The Northern Lights dance across the heavens like utterly silent fireworks. They are caused by solar winds: eruptions on the sun release charged particles into space, which are drawn toward the Earth by its magnetic fields. The magnetic North and South Poles, in particular, pull the particles into the Earth's atmosphere, where they react with gases. The gases become illuminated and different colors appear in the sky. The Northern Lights are seldom visible in the more temperate latitudes, since the magnetic fields there are not strong enough.

At low tide (*above*), large areas of fjords and bays are left high and dry. In such locations, a sailboat needs to be secured with mooring lines and two anchors, since the tide returns with enormous force twice each day.

225

Leaving a backpack unattended in an area where bears reside (*previous pages*) is not a good idea. Bears are extremely curious and are interested in any new object that appears in their territory. Losing pieces of equipment in the wilderness can seriously endanger a person's chances of survival.

Camping in bear territory is always risky, since there are only a few truly effective methods for keeping bears away from a campsite. A portable electric fence is the most effective and practical solution. Scattering moth balls—a scent bears despise—in the area has only a limited effect. It is absolutely essential not to store any food—including toothpaste or lotion—in your tent. The only safe way to store these items is in a bite-proof container that bears cannot open. Once bears have discovered food at a campsite, they pose a very real danger for the campers. They will repeatedly attempt to plunder the tents, particularly when there are no people present.

BACKGROUND
INFORMATION

Name: Brown bear, Grizzly bear (in North America)
Scientific name: *Ursus arctos*
Height: Varies widely according to geographic area; 35–60 in (90–160 cm) at the shoulder or 5–9 ft (160–280 cm) standing on hind legs
Weight: Varies widely with geographic area; females 175–550 lb (80–250 kg), males 300–1200 lb (140–550 kg)
Life expectancy: 25 to max. 40 years
Reproduction: Mating period May to June; delayed implantation of egg cells. Gestation period (including egg cell dormancy) lasts 7–8 months; fetal growth period only ca. 60 days. Have 1 to 4 cubs (2 is average)
Diet: Omnivorous; may be primarily vegetarian depending on geographic region
Habitat: Coastal regions, open tundra, light taiga forests, mountains up to 11,500 ft (3500 m)
Geographic range: Northern hemisphere, northern Canada, Alaska, Siberia, the Himalayas, Central Asia, Scandinavia, southeastern Europe; worldwide population approximately 185,000–200,000 animals

Name: American black bear or Baribal
Scientific name: *Ursus americanus*
Height: 27–35 in (70–90 cm) at shoulder; 55–70 in (140–180 cm) standing on hind legs
Weight: Females 110–175 lb (50–80 kg), males 130–550 lb (60–250 kg)
Life expectancy: Approximately 30 years
Reproduction: Mating period May to July. Gestation (including egg cell dormancy) lasts 7–8 months; fetal growth period is only 60–70 days. Have 2 or 3 cubs.
Diet: Primarily vegetarian (over 75%); otherwise insects, small mammals and carrion
Habitat: Forests with thick undergrowth, scrubland
Geographic range: Most of North America and Alaska, Canada except for the extreme north, south into the Mexican mountain ranges. Population: over 700,000

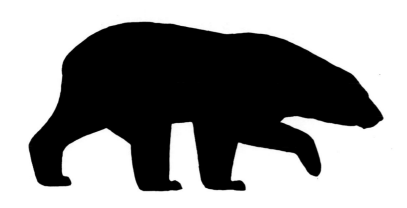

Name: Polar bear

Scientific name: *Ursus maritimus*

Height: 55–63 in (140–160 cm) at shoulder; 6.5–8 ft (2–2.5 m) standing on hind legs

Weight: Females, 330–660 lb (150–300 kg), males 925–1300 lb (420–600 kg)

Life expectancy: 20 to 30 years

Reproduction: Mating period March to May. Gestation (including dormancy) ca. 8 months. Average 2 cubs

Diet: Carnivorous, primarily seals, fish and sea birds.

Habitat and range: Drift and pack ice of the Arctic Ocean and coasts in entire North Pole region: northern Canada, Alaska, Greenland, Svalbard and the Russian Arctic. Worldwide population is ca. 20,000 to 25,000.

THE BEAR FAMILY TREE

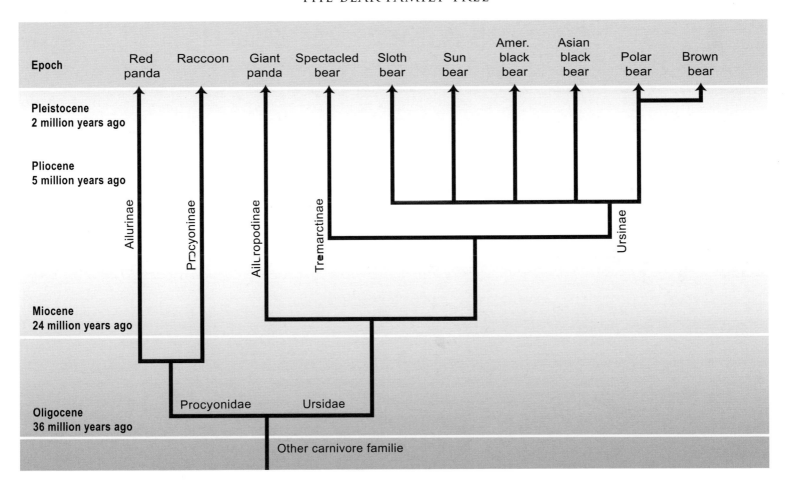

All living predators can trace their ancestry back to small, bamboo-dwelling carnivores, the miacids, which existed about 50 million years ago. These animals gave rise to the two major classifications of carnivores, the "cat-like" (*Feloidea* or *Aeluroidea*) and the "dog-like" (*Canoidea*). Bears are classified among the suborder of dog-like animals. As opposed to the small bears (Procyonidae), the large bears are classified as "true bears," with giant pandas and spectacled bears occupying special categories.

The map on the following pages illustrates the approximate geographic distribution of the large bear species today. In the past hundred years, the original geographic distribution of nearly all the bear species has shrunk dramatically. The primary reason for this is destruction of their habitats by human beings. Thanks to protective measures such as national parks, regulated hunting, and research projects, some populations have stabilized once again, or even increased their numbers slightly.

Greenland

Iceland

Nor

Alaska

Pacific

Ocean

C a n a d a

Denmark

Ireland

United
Kingdom

1 Ger

2

Luxbou

France

3

Atlantic

Ocean

United States

of America

Portugal

Spain

Gibraltar

Mexico

Bahamas

Morocco

Cuba

Western Sahara

Algeria

Haiti

Dominican
Republic

Belize

Netherlands
Antilles

Honduras Jamaica

Guatemala

Puerto Rico

Mauritania

Mali

El Salvador

Caribbean

Caribbean
Islands

Nicaragua

Senegal

Costa Rica

Venezuela

Guyana

Gambia

Burkina
Faso

Ni

Panama

Suriname

Guinea-Bissau

Guinea

Colombia

French
Guyana

Sierra Leone

Ivory
Coast

Ecuador

Liberia

Togo

Peru

Ghana Benin

Equatorial
Guinea

B r a z i l

Atlantic

Ocean

Bolivia

1   Netherland
2   Belgium
3   Switzerland
4   Austria
5   Slovenia
6   Croatia
7   Czech Republic
8   Slovakia
9   Bosnia and Herzegovina
10 Serbia
11 Macedonia
12 Albania
13 Montenegro
14 Bulgaria
15 Greece
16 Moldavia
17 Lebanon
18 Israel
19 Jordan
20 Georgia
21 Armenia
22 Azerbaijan

Para-
guay

Chile

Pacific

Ocean

Argentina

Uru-
guay

A n t a r c t i c

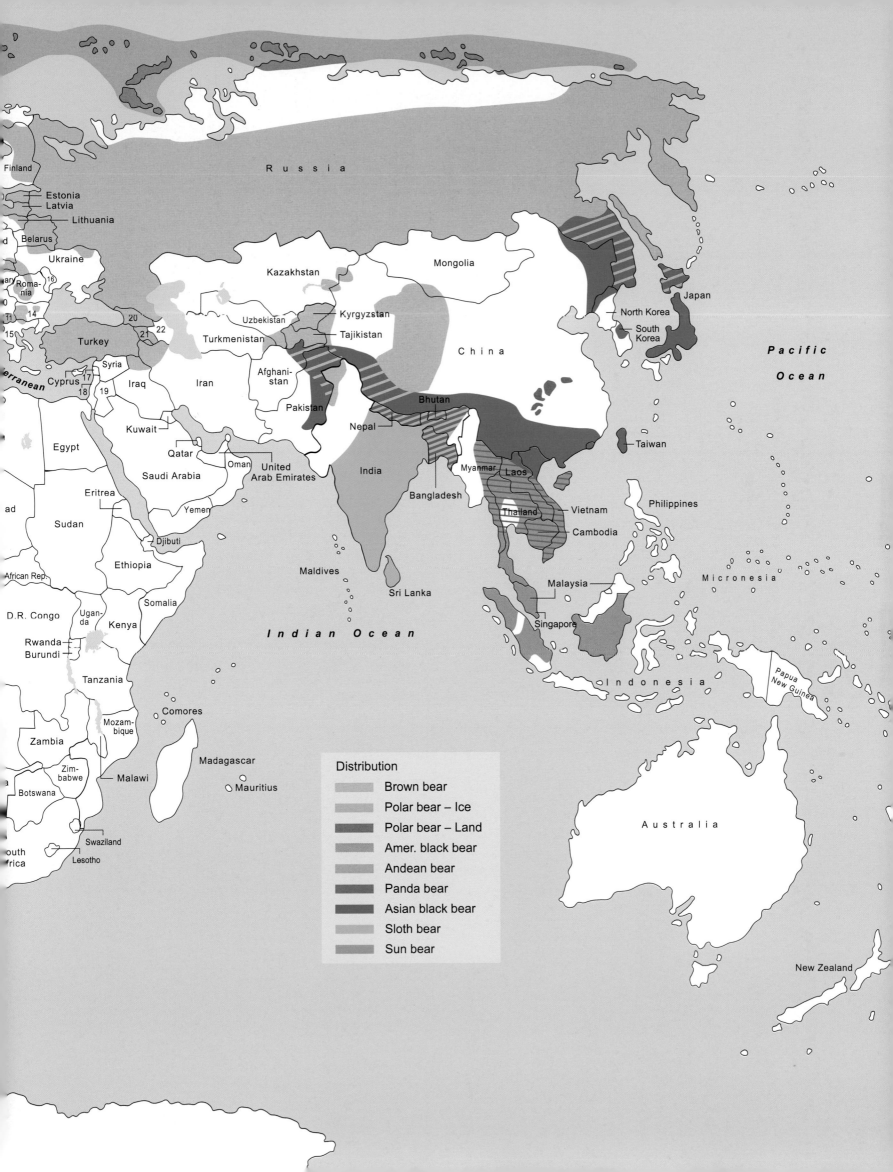

Finland

Estonia
Latvia
Lithuania
Belarus
Ukraine
Roma-
nia
16
14
11
15
20
Turkey
21
22
Cyprus
17
18
19
Syria
Iraq
Mediterranean

R u s s i a

Kazakhstan

Mongolia

Uzbekistan
Kyrgyzstan
Turkmenistan
Tajikistan

Afghani-
stan

Pakistan

Iran

China

North Korea
South
Korea

Japan

Pacific

Ocean

Bhutan
Nepal

Taiwan

Kuwait
Qatar
Oman
United
Arab Emirates
Saudi Arabia
Yemen

India

Myanmar
Laos

Bangladesh

Thailand
Vietnam
Cambodia

Philippines

Egypt

Eritrea

Sudan

Ethiopia

Djibouti

Maldives

Sri Lanka

I n d i a n   O c e a n

M i c r o n e s i a

Malaysia

Singapore

African Rep.

D.R. Congo
Uganda
da
Kenya
Rwanda
Burundi

Somalia

I n d o n e s i a

Papua
New
Guinea

Tanzania

Comores

Mozam-
bique

Madagascar

Mauritius

Zambia

Zimbabwe
Malawi

Botswana

Australia

Swaziland

outh
frica
Lesotho

Distribution

Brown bear

Polar bear – Ice

Polar bear – Land

Amer. black bear

Andean bear

Panda bear

Asian black bear

Sloth bear

Sun bear

New Zealand

In contrast to brown bears, polar bears (*above*), which are almost exclusively carnivorous, have the dentition of predators, including sharp molars. Except for the pads (*below right*), even the soles of their feet are completely covered with fur as protection against the cold. Each paw has five toes with non-retractable claws. The polar bear's paws are very wide, which serves the purpose of distributing their substantial body weight over a larger area. This is ideal, allowing them to walk even on thin ice, which does not break readily underneath them.

The cave bear (*above right*) was a true giant, the heaviest species of bear that ever existed on earth. An utterly successful example of evolution, the cave bear became extinct approximately 15,000 years ago, at the same time as the mammoth and the woolly rhinoceros. The cave bear's body mass was 33 percent greater than that of today's brown bears; its geographic range extended throughout the non-frozen regions of Europe and the Near East. Its name is derived from the fact that large numbers of cave bear skeletons have been found in naturally occurring caves, where the bears apparently hibernated. During the Middle Ages, when people discovered these enormous skulls, they thought they were the skulls of dragons. Thus originated the legend of a fire-breathing dragon that lives in caves in many regions.

THE PHOTOGRAPHER AND AUTHOR

1959 Born in Gotha, Thuringian Forest, East Germany

1976 Dramatic escape to West Germany via former Czechoslovakia and Austria; was shot at by border guards while swimming across the Danube River

1977–1980 Trained as a sailor on overseas trade ships around the world

1984 Traveled across Greenland, photographing polar bears for the first time in Upernavik

1985 Certification as a game warden

1988–1989 Worked as a forest consultant in China, India and Pakistan

1989 Mountain bike tour through the Himalayas

1991 Yukon River expedition: Traveled 2,000 miles (3,200 km) by canoe through northern Canada and Alaska

1993 Climbed Alaska's Mount McKinley with complete complement of filming gear

1996 First cameraman in the world to film a wild grizzly bear under water

2003 3-month-long sailboat expedition observing Kodiak bears on the Aleutian Islands with his 9-year-old son, Erik

2005 Repeated Yukon River expedition with his family.

2006 Several mountain gorilla expeditions in central Africa.

2006 Expedition in the Tian Shan Mountains in search of snow leopards and Marco Polo sheep.

2007 Expedition to study saltwater crocodiles in northern Australia; diving with a crocodile.

2007 Expedition to study Komodo dragons in eastern Indonesia.

2008 Lecture tours in India, the Arabian Peninsula and Germany.

Documentary filmmaker since **1990** (selected works)

1992 *2000 Meilen Freiheit (2,000 Miles of Freedom)*, A canoe expedition on the Yukon River—from the source to the Bering Sea, 2-part film, ARD Television

1993 *Die Waljäger von Point Hope (The Whale Hunters of Point Hope)*, WDR Television

1994 *Polar Bears—Arctic Rulers*, ZDF Television
Der Uhu—Jäger der Nacht (Eagle Owls—Hunters of the Night), WDR Television

1995 *Der Mount McKinley—Ein eiskaltes Abenteuer (Mount McKinley—An Ice-Cold Adventure)*, ARD Television

1995 *Knast für Eisbären (A Prison for Polar Bears)*, WDR Television

1995–1997 *Im Schatten der Gletscher (In the Shadow of the Glacier)*, ZDF Television, co-production with Discovery Channel

1998–1999 *In the Depths of the Forest*, ZDF Television, co-production with Discovery Channel

1999–2001 *Nomads of the North*, ZDF Television, co-production with Discovery Channel

2002–2003 *Giant Grizzlies*, ZDF Television, co-production with Discovery Channel and Animal Planet Special

2003–2004 *The Bear Man*, ARD Television, co-production with National Geographic

2004–2006 *Abenteuer Yukon River (Yukon River Adventure)*, 3-part series, ARD Television, co-production with National Geographic and Arte

Part 1: *Durch das wilde Herz Kanadas (Through the Wild Heart of Canada)*

Part 2: *Auf den Spuren der Goldsucher (On the Trail of the Gold Seekers)*

Part 3: *Der lange Weg bis zum Eismeer (The Long Journey to the Arctic Ocean)*

2006–2008 *Die letzten ihrer Art—Magische Momente (The Last of Their Kind—Magic Moments)*, 3-part series, ZDF Television, co-production with National Geographic and Arte

Part 1: *Durch Hochgebirge und Urwälder (Through High Mountains and Rainforests)*

Part 2: *Durch Eis und Wüste (Through Ice and Deserts)*

Part 3: *In Ozeanen und Sümpfen (In Oceans and Swamps)*

2007 *Im Visier der Grizzly Giganten (On the Trail of the Giant Grizzlies)*, ZDF Television

EXPEDITIONS: 1984–2007

INDEX

For my Alaskan friends Steven Nourse and Greg A.
Syverson, with whom I had the privilege of sharing so
many fantastic adventures in the northern wilderness!
And in memory of photographers Michio Hoshino,
Timothy Treadwell and Vitaly Nikolayenko, who
loved the bears as much as I do.

I would like to thank the following for their support
on my many expeditions:
Perry and Angela Mollan, Nick Jans, John Bartolino,
Charly Hall, Steven Kazlowski, Eberhard Brunner,
Shauna and Parker Fitzpatrick, Ryan Hill, Wolfgang
Hebel, Paul J. Hansen, Otto and Hanni Zimmermann,
Rachel Syverson, Marty and Marion Owen, Don and
Jennifer Ciancio, Matthias Breiter, Victor van Ballen-
berghe, David Neel Jr., Heather Johnson, Frank
Gutsche, Karry and Sascha O'Neil, Birgit Kieling,
Kay Kesling, and the University of Alaska Fairbanks.

This is a Parragon Publishing Book

Copyright © Parragon Books Ltd

Parragon Books Ltd
Queen Street House
4 Queen Street
Bath BA1 1HE, UK

All Photographs © Andreas Kieling
© Steven Nourse (74, 170, 171, 218/219, 234/235), Henriette Lavaulx-
Vrecourt (14, 15), Oakley Chochran (236), Greg A. Syverson (9, 223),
Erik Kieling (10, 11, 12, 82, 120, 121, 218 top)

Original edition: Daniela Kumor, Cologne
Maps and graphics: Burga Fillery, Berlin

Copyright © 2008 Parragon Books Ltd for the English edition
English edition produced by: APE Int'l, Richmond, VA
Translation from German: Mary Dobrian for APE Int'l

ISBN 978-1-4075-4157-0

Printed in China